DK SUPER History

SALEM WITCH TRIALS

Delve into the background, events and aftermath of America's deadliest witch hunt

PRODUCED FOR DK BY
Editorial Just Content Limited
Design Studio Noel

Author Nick Hunter

Senior Editor Ankita Awasthi Tröger
Editor Hattie Hansford
Senior Art Editor Gilda Pacitti
Graphic Story Illustrator Matt Garbutt
Managing Editor Carine Tracanelli
Managing Art Editor Sarah Corcoran
Pre-Production Coordinator Shanker Prasad
Pre-Production Designer Jaypal Chauhan
Production Controller Rebecca Parton
Publisher Sarah Forbes
Managing Director, Learning Hilary Fine

First published in Great Britain in 2025 by
Dorling Kindersley Limited
20 Vauxhall Bridge Road,
London SW1V 2SA

The authorised representative in the EEA is
Dorling Kindersley Verlag GmbH. Arnulfstr. 124,
80636 Munich, Germany

10 9 8 7 6 5 4 3 2 1
001–345325–Sep/2025

A CIP catalogue record for this book
is available from the British Library.
ISBN: 978-0-2417-2082-0

Printed and bound in China

www.dk.com

This book was made with Forest Stewardship Council™ certified paper – one small step in DK's commitment to a sustainable future.
Learn more at www.dk.com/uk/information/sustainability

Contents

Words in **bold** are explained in the glossary on page 44.

History in Perspective

In the winter of 1692, the people of Salem Village, Massachusetts, were shaken by a mystery illness. The illness mainly affected young women. It was blamed on **witchcraft**. This led to a series of events that divided this deeply religious community.

Puritans believed in witchcraft. They thought that witches worked with the **Devil** and used magic to harm people.

Where and when?

Salem Village was part of the province of Massachusetts Bay, a **colony** founded in 1630 by **settlers** from England. These settlers followed a strict form of Christianity. They were known as Puritans. The government and laws of the colony were based on the rules of their religion. The small European colonies on North America's coasts were surrounded by **Indigenous** populations. They were often mistreated by the settlers.

Think about it

We know about the Salem witch **trials** from various **sources** written at the time. Most of these sources were written by men. Why might they not give us a full picture of what happened?

Everyone in the Puritan community was expected to attend church. This picture shows them walking through the snow on their way to **worship**. The Bible was important to the Puritans and they spent a lot of their free time reading it. They closely followed its teachings, as they believed it would help them live good lives.

Who was involved?

Massachusetts was mostly **governed** by Puritan men. The events of the Salem witch trials affected mainly women and girls, but they had very little power, as men made most of the decisions. Non-Puritans also had less influence in the community.

Different perspectives

Different groups in society may have deeply contrasting experiences of events. Official records of the past often only present one side of the story. This means that they can't reflect the experiences of everyone affected. To understand what happened, it is important that we look at events from more than one point of view.

Key Events

WHAT HAPPENED WHEN

The Salem witch trials spread fear and **suspicion** through the community in 1692. This terrible sequence of events claimed the lives of many **innocent** people.

1692

JANUARY

Several young girls start having **fits** and outbursts of screaming. Doctor William Griggs says the girls have been **bewitched**.

1 MARCH

Three women appear before local **magistrates**. Sarah Good, Sarah Osborne and Tituba are **accused** of using witchcraft to cause the mystery illness.

27 MAY

As several more people are accused, **Governor** William Phips issues orders for a special court to be set up.

2 JUNE

Bridget Bishop's trial begins. She becomes the first person in Salem to be **executed** for being a witch.

19 SEPTEMBER

Giles Corey is executed for refusing to accept the court's decision. His wife Martha is executed a few days later. Salem's people start to turn against the witch trials.

29 OCTOBER

Governor William Phips ends the special court. A new court is set up. A lot of the **evidence** against the accused was based on dreams and **visions**, but this is not allowed in the new court.

1693

9 MAY

Tituba undergoes trial and is released. Governor William Phips **pardons** everyone who is still imprisoned for witchcraft.

1711

17 OCTOBER

The colonial government of Massachusetts passes a bill clearing most of the people found guilty in the Salem witch trials.

Key People
WHO'S WHO

The Salem witch trials affected hundreds of people in Salem Village and across colonial Massachusetts.

The accused

Tituba
An enslaved Indigenous woman who was part of **Minister** Samuel Parris's household. Tituba helped look after his children. She was the first to be accused of witchcraft. She spent over a year in jail.

Sarah Good

Sarah Good
A poor woman who was not well-liked in the village. She was one of the first people to be accused of witchcraft. She was executed.

Sarah Osborne
An unwell and unpopular woman accused at the same time as Sarah Good. She died in jail.

Bridget Bishop
An **innkeeper** who was the first person to be executed for witchcraft in 1692.

Martha and Giles Corey
Martha Corey was one of the first church members to be accused. Giles Corey refused to accept the court's decision. They were both accused of witchcraft and executed.

The affected

Elizabeth (Betty) Parris
The 9-year-old daughter of Minister Samuel Parris.

Abigail Williams
Betty's cousin, the 11-year-old niece of Minister Samuel Parris.

Elizabeth Hubbard
A 17-year-old girl who accused others of witchcraft.

Ann Putnam
The 12-year-old daughter of a powerful and important Salem family. She was the accuser of many of the victims.

People of authority

Samuel Parris
The minister of Salem Village.

Sir William Phips
The governor of Massachusetts, who ordered a special court to be set up for the witchcraft trials.

William Stoughton
The chief **judge** in the witch trials.

John Hathorne and Samuel Sewall
Local magistrates who served as judges in the Salem witch trials.

Increase Mather
The minister and president of Harvard College. He helped end the trials.

Samuel Parris

Key Location

SALEM VILLAGE

In the late 17th century there were two places called Salem. Salem Town was a busy port on Massachusetts Bay, and is the place now known as Salem. A short distance away was Salem Village. This was a farming community of about 500 people and is now the town of Danvers. The accusations of witchcraft, investigations and questioning took place in Salem Village. The trials took place in Salem Town.

REBECCA NURSE'S HOMESTEAD

The home of Rebecca Nurse, one of the most well-known victims of the witch trials. Rebecca was a 71-year-old grandmother and a respected member of the Salem community when she was accused of witchcraft and convicted and executed. Rebecca is believed to be buried here and it now operates as a museum.

SALEM VILLAGE PARSONAGE

The home of Minister Samuel Parris, the minister of Salem Village. This was the first place where his daughter Betty and niece Abigail Williams showed strange behavior. Tituba, an enslaved woman in the Parris household, was one of the first people to be accused. She **confessed** under pressure.

PROCTOR'S LEDGE/GALLOWS HILL

The site of the **gallows** where 19 people accused of witchcraft were executed by hanging. For a long time it was not known exactly where these took place. But research and **archaeological evidence** found that it was near the base of Gallows Hill, known as Proctor's Ledge.

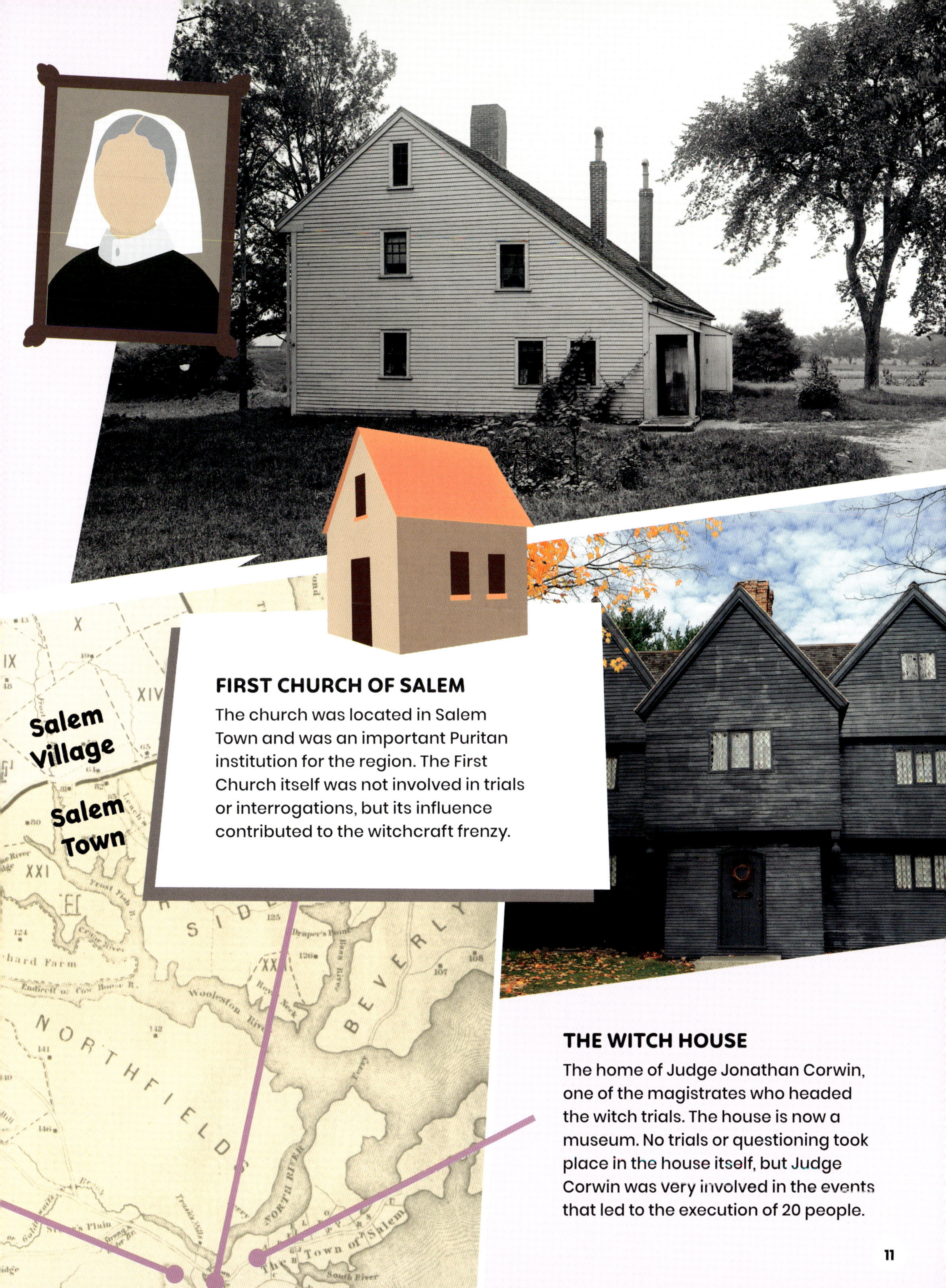

FIRST CHURCH OF SALEM

The church was located in Salem Town and was an important Puritan institution for the region. The First Church itself was not involved in trials or interrogations, but its influence contributed to the witchcraft frenzy.

THE WITCH HOUSE

The home of Judge Jonathan Corwin, one of the magistrates who headed the witch trials. The house is now a museum. No trials or questioning took place in the house itself, but Judge Corwin was very involved in the events that led to the execution of 20 people.

Salem in Crisis

In January 1692, Doctor William Griggs was asked to rush to the home of Minister Samuel Parris in Salem Village. When he arrived, he found two young girls screaming loudly and having fits. The doctor shocked everyone by saying they had been bewitched.

Over 200 people, mainly women, were accused of being witches.

WITCH HUNT

Many people already believed that witchcraft could cause illness, so the doctor's findings created fear throughout the village. In the following weeks, suspected witches were accused of bewitching the girls. They were arrested and put on trial. Over the summer of 1692, many people were dragged into the crisis.

Massachusetts Bay was one of several small colonies on the east coast of North America. This map shows Old Reading, another nearby part of the Massachusetts Bay colony.

VILLAGE TENSIONS

The small community of Salem Village was divided. Some residents attended the church led by the new minister, Samuel Parris. Others did not. Families often argued over land ownership and changes in the community. Wars between England and France and conflicts with Indigenous communities brought more people to the area. The Puritans felt threatened by these newcomers.

Think about it

If you were sick and went to the doctor, they would try to find out what was wrong with you and make you better. What does the doctor's **diagnosis** say about medical knowledge in the 1600s?

PURITAN COMMUNITY

Puritans believed witchcraft was a sign that God was displeased. So they were frightened by the idea that there might be witches in their community.

Belief in Witchcraft

The people of Salem were not the only people who believed in witches and witchcraft. Witch trials had taken place in Europe for hundreds of years. Settlers from England brought their beliefs about witches to Massachusetts.

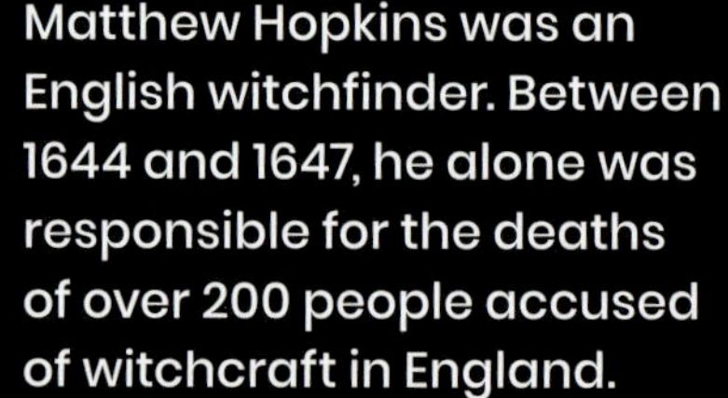

Matthew Hopkins was an English witchfinder. Between 1644 and 1647, he alone was responsible for the deaths of over 200 people accused of witchcraft in England.

Fascinating fact

From 1400 to about 1750, around 3 in every 4 people accused of witchcraft were women. **Medieval** books on identifying witches focused on women. They were usually written by men.

WHAT WAS A WITCH?

Witch trials first started in Europe during the 1400s. They became common in the late 1500s and early 1600s. Thousands of people were executed for witchcraft during this time. Many Christians believed that witches worked with the Devil, who gave them **supernatural** powers. People believed that witches could change from human to animal form. They also believed that witches used animal helpers known as "familiars".

WITCHCRAFT AND THE LAW

Witchcraft was an **offence** in the Massachusetts Bay colony. Anyone found to be guilty of witchcraft could be executed. Before the Salem witch trials, this was a rare occurrence. But in 1688, Ann Glover was found guilty and executed for bewitching several young girls in Boston, Massachusetts.

Witches are often pictured with black cats. But people believed other animals could also be their familiars. At least two dogs were executed during the Salem witch trials.

WITCH TESTS

People held various beliefs about how to identify witches. For example, when a person saw the witch who had bewitched them, they were supposed to scream or appear in pain. This was used as evidence as the witch trials unfolded in Salem. In Salem, there are reports that Tituba helped make "witch cake" to find the witches. Urine from the bewitched girls was mixed with oatmeal and baked. This "cake" was fed to a dog. It was hoped that the dog would fall under the spell of the witch and somehow reveal the witch's name.

Illness and Accusations

When Doctor William Griggs decided that the mystery illness was due to witchcraft, people wanted to find out who was to blame. The witch hunt became more urgent as other girls also started to get sick. New cases included Ann Putnam, the daughter of a well-known local family.

Sarah Good, also known as Granny Good, was found guilty of being a witch.

WITCH HUNT

Minister Samuel Parris held prayer meetings to help his daughter and niece, who were acting strangely. Salem's leaders asked the two girls who they thought had bewitched them. The girls named three people as witches. The first was Tituba, an enslaved Indigenous woman in the Parris home. The second was Sarah Good, a poor woman who was not well-liked in the village. The third was Sarah Osborne, an older woman who did not attend church often. These three women were among the first in Salem to be accused of witchcraft.

Tituba was one of the women accused of witchcraft.

This picture presents Tituba as frightening children. Remember that artists can create dramatic images that do not show reality.

INVESTIGATION

Local magistrates questioned the three women. When the girls saw the women in the courtroom, they screamed and appeared to be in pain. Sarah Osborne and Sarah Good strongly denied being witches. When Minister Samuel Parris forced Tituba to confess, she said there were other witches in Salem.

Think about it

The first women to be accused were all outsiders, either because of their background or the way they behaved. Why do you think people blamed them?

The Spread of Panic

The strange illness that sparked the witchcraft rumours kept spreading. Ann Putnam, her mother, her cousin and their servant also got sick. As a result of Tituba's confession, people believed there were more witches in the village. By the end of March 1692, it seemed like anyone in the community could be suspected of witchcraft.

Within a few weeks, prison cells were overflowing with people accused of witchcraft. Judges asked for outside help to handle the huge scale of the Salem witch trials.

NEW SUSPECTS

Before long, suspicion began turning to respected members of society. Martha Corey was a faithful member of the church community. This did not stop young Ann Putnam from accusing her of witchcraft. Rebecca Nurse was a well-known older woman. Dorcas Good was the young daughter of Sarah Good. They were both accused of witchcraft. Some men were also accused, including Martha Corey's husband, Giles Corey.

People talked about who might be a witch in the church meeting house.

COMMUNITY DISPUTES

Most accusations came from a small number of people. Ann Putnam alone accused over 60 people of witchcraft. Suspected witches often accused others of being involved. They hoped this would help their own case when they said they were innocent.

Fascinating fact

The illness that led to accusations of witchcraft remains a mystery. Some scientists believe it was caused by a fungus that grew on bread. This might explain why it spread across the community. But it does not explain why most of the sick were girls and women. It has also been suggested that **mass hysteria** could have contributed to the events in Salem.

A New Court Convenes

By May 1692, the witchcraft accusations had spiralled out of control. More than 100 people were now facing **charges**. Sir William Phips, the new governor of Massachusetts, had to act quickly. He ordered a special court to be set up in Salem.

Sir William Phips

THE SPECIAL COURT

The court was set up to listen to and decide on witchcraft cases. The main judge was William Stoughton, one of the colony's top **officials**. People brought to the court faced a tough choice. If they admitted to witchcraft and named other witches, they got a lighter punishment. If they denied they were a witch but were found guilty, they could be executed.

The new court was powerful. It included judges from outside Salem. Some of them had been involved in an earlier witch trial. This made some people wonder if the accused would get fair trials.

Although he had no formal legal training, William Stoughton was a judge during the trials.

The Wonders of the Invisible World:

Being an Account of the

TRYALS

OF

Several Witches,

Lately Excuted in

NEW-ENGLAND:

And of feveral remarkable Curiofities therein Occurring.

Together with,

I. Obfervations upon the Nature, the Number, and the Operations of the Devils.
II. A fhort Narrative of a late outrage committed by a knot of Witches in *Swede-Land*, very much refembling, and fo far explaining, that under which *New-England* has laboured.
III. Some Councels directing a due Improvement of the Terrible things lately done by the unufual and amazing Range of *Evil-Spirits* in *New-England.*
IV. A brief Difcourfe upon thofe *Temptations* which are the more ordinary Devices of Satan.

By COTTON MATHER.

Publifhed by the Special Command of his EXCELLENCY the Govenour of the Province of the *Maffachufetts-Bay* in *New-England.*

Printed firft, at *Boftun* in *New-England*; and Reprinted at *London*, for *John Dunton*, at the *Raven* in the *Poultry*. 1693.

COTTON MATHER

Cotton Mather was an important Puritan leader. His book, *The Wonders of the Invisible World*, tells the story of many of the trials. Mather claimed the book was not **biased**, and he did have some doubts about the trials. However, he was very **critical** of some of the victims. For example, he described Susannah North Martin as “one of the most... wicked creatures in the world” (Mather, 1692).

Fascinating fact

Just like this one, most of the documents written during the Salem witch trials still exist. They help us learn about the trials and the people involved. For example, most settlers in colonial **New England** could read and write, which was very unusual at the time.

Under Suspicion

Martha Corey
Devout Puritan woman

Giles Corey
Farmer and husband of Martha Corey

Ann Putnam
12-year-old daughter of the well-known Putnam family

Ann Putnam Sr
Mother of the younger Ann

Edward Putnam
Investigator and Ann's uncle

Ezekiel Cheever
Investigator and clerk of the court

John Hathorne
Salem merchant and magistrate, a leading judge in the trials

Salem Village, March 1692. Martha Corey was a respected member of the community when stories began to be shared of girls being bewitched.

Martha, there are accusations of witchcraft in the village.

The villagers grew suspicious of anyone who did not join in the hunt for witches, but Martha wanted no involvement in the stories of witchcraft.

Across Salem Village, people wanted to know why girls were falling ill.
Ann Putnam was one of the first girls to fall ill.
There must be more witches causing this. Perhaps your uncle can help us.
Niece, tell us who has bewitched you.
In my dream, the witch torments me, pinching and hitting me.
What does she wear?
She blinded me so I could not see, but I heard her name – Martha Corey.
Oh! She pretended to be so godly!

Edward Putnam and his fellow investigator Ezekiel Cheever went to question Martha Corey.
I know why you are here. You have come to accuse me of being a witch.
A girl says you have visited her as a witch in her dream.
Do you speak of your niece Ann, Mr Putnam? Did you ask her what clothes I wore?
The two men were shocked by Martha's questions.
How do you know we asked her this? Ann says you blinded her in her dream so she could not see.
It is no witchcraft. I know because I have heard people talking.
Despite Martha's denial, the men were sure that she was involved in witchcraft.
She knew our questions before we even asked them. How else can we explain that?

As word spread, there were more accusations.
How does this witch dare to sit among us?
Have you heard? Martha Corey is to be arrested!
If a godly woman like Martha is suspected, then no one is safe!
After the church meeting, Martha was arrested.
Judge Hathorne was in charge of Martha's trial.
Admit that you bewitched these girls!
I am an innocent woman. I have never had anything to do with witchcraft.
Martha was found guilty despite no real evidence.

Who Was Accused?

Over the course of 1692, more than 200 people were charged with witchcraft in Salem Village. Most of the people who were targeted were women who were seen as outsiders in this strict Puritan community. Several men were also accused, along with others from nearby towns across the Massachusetts Bay colony. This period was marked by fear and suspicion. Many innocent people were blamed for things they did not do.

Pillories hold a prisoner's arms in place and stocks hold their legs. We do not know for certain that these were used in Salem, but it is likely as they were often used as public punishment at the time.

BEYOND SALEM

The victims of the trials were not just from Salem. Susannah North Martin lived in nearby Amesbury and had already been accused of witchcraft in the past. Now, four girls claimed she had visited them in a dream and told them her name. The judges saw this as evidence of witchcraft and she was found guilty and executed.

Fascinating fact

In 2022, part of Interstate 495 was renamed the Susannah North Martin Highway to honour Susannah.

A Modeſt Enquiry
Into the Nature of
Witchcraft,
AND
How Perſons Guilty of that Crime may be *Convicted*: And the means uſed for their Diſcovery Diſcuſſed, both *Negatively* and *Affirmatively*, according to SCRIPTURE and EXPERIENCE.

By John Hale,
Paſtor of the C… Chriſt in *Beverley*,
…697.

SELF-DEFENCE

Margaret Jacobs accused her own grandfather, George Jacobs. She had already been accused of witchcraft. Like many of the victims, Margaret may have named George to avoid execution. George was executed, though Margaret was not. She later took back her accusation against him.

John Hale was a minister in nearby Beverley. He supported the trials until his wife was accused. He later published a book about the trials.

BRIDGET BISHOP

Bridget Bishop was well known in the community for wearing fine, colourful clothes and acting in a way that broke the strict rules of the Puritan religion. She had been accused of witchcraft in the past, and was now found guilty of it. Bridget was executed on 10 June 1692, the first victim of the witch trials.

Family Feuds

During the events in Salem, the Putnam family was involved in several of the accusations. Some members of the family, such as young Ann Putnam, became ill and accused people of being witches. Ann's father, Thomas Putnam, helped with the investigations and trials. Many people think the Putnams might have used these accusations to punish their enemies in the village.

These actors are performing as Thomas and Ann Putnam Sr in a 1960s play about the witch trials of Salem.

The Putnams lived in a big house in Salem Village.

A DIVIDED VILLAGE

The Putnam family was very important in Salem Village. They owned a lot of land and helped run the community. They wanted the village to have its own church and minister, separate from the bigger town of Salem. The Putnams were strict Puritans who supported Minister Samuel Parris. They did not get along with another wealthy family called the Porters, and the two families fought over who should control the village.

GEORGE BURROUGHS

George Burroughs was a former minister in Salem Village. He had borrowed money from the Putnam family, leading to a long-standing **grudge** between them. George had moved away from Salem, but was brought back to face trial. He was accused of leading the witches. Many local people spoke against him. Just before he was executed, he said the **Lord's Prayer**. People believed witches could not do this, so some called for him to be pardoned.

Think about it

Many enemies of the Putnam family were killed or imprisoned during the witch trials. Do you think the Putnams could have caused these events to happen on purpose?

A picture that imagines the scene of George Burrows saying the Lord's Prayer before he was executed.

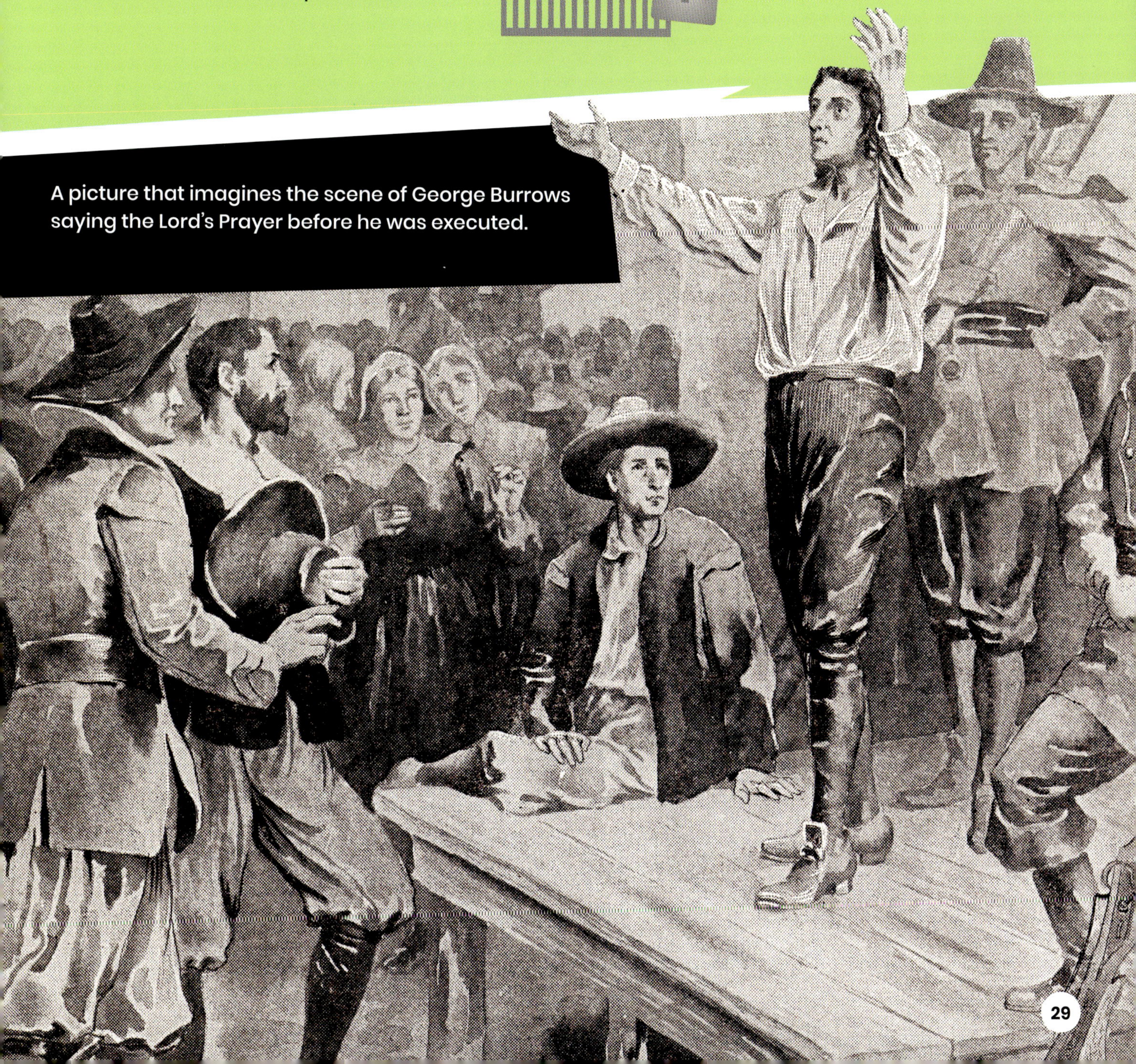

Justice and Fairness

The **right** to a fair trial is very important. If a person is accused of **committing** a crime, this right means they will be treated fairly. There were lots of problems with the way the Salem witch trials were managed, and many people question whether the trials were fair.

PRESUMED GUILTY

According to the law, people should be considered innocent until proven guilty. But this was not the case in Salem. During the trials, people automatically assumed a suspected witch was guilty. The accused did not have access to a **defence lawyer** to question witnesses and find mistakes in trial evidence. This support did not exist.

SPECTRAL EVIDENCE

Accusers of suspected witches claimed the witch had visited them in a dream or vision. As a result, no one else could have seen them. This was known as "spectral evidence". It was impossible to **disprove**. The Puritan leader Cotton Mather said this evidence should be treated carefully. But it was still used in the trials. His father, Increase Mather, did not agree with using this kind of evidence.

The document below lists people who accused Sarah Good of witchcraft. It includes Abigail Williams and Ann Putnam. Sarah Good had no defence lawyer to question these witnesses.

Increase Mather seemed to be more concerned with justice than his son. Increase said, "It were better that ten suspected witches should escape, than that one innocent person should be **condemned**" (Mather, 1693).

Think about it

Can you think of other reasons why the trials may have been unfair? Who was judging the trials? How were they organised?

Trials Opposed

Most people in Salem Village believed in the power of witchcraft. But not everyone supported the way the trials were handled. As the trials continued into the autumn of 1692, more people questioned what was happening. However, as several people discovered, anyone who **opposed** the trials risked being accused themselves.

AUTHORITIES OBJECTED

Nathaniel Saltonstall was a judge in the special court. He resigned after Bridget Bishop was found guilty because he was **outraged** by the way the court worked. Several other ministers also objected to the use of spectral evidence.

THE RISKS OF PROTEST

John Willard was Salem Village's **deputy constable**. He opposed the witch trials by refusing to arrest people he believed were innocent. He was soon accused of witchcraft himself. A relative claimed John Willard had made him ill, and the Putnam family accused him of causing the death of one of their children many years before. John Willard was executed in August 1692. Another man called John Proctor was also found guilty and executed after he spoke out against the trials.

A memorial for John Proctor at the Salem Witch Trials Memorial. After his death, John was cleared of the charges of witchcraft.

SILENCING WOMEN

Men like John Willard and John Proctor knew there were great risks in speaking out. In a society and court **dominated** by men, it was even more difficult for women to speak out against the witch trials. Their only option was to insist they were innocent.

Joseph Putnam, the youngest brother of Thomas, opposed the trials. He spoke out against them as he didn't believe in witchcraft, unlike the rest of his family. He kept a horse ready at all times to escape if accused himself.

Think about it

Why do you think the women and girls of Salem accused others of being witches? Some later admitted that their stories were not true. What reasons can you think of to explain why they didn't tell the truth?

Women in the Puritan religion were expected to **defer** to men and look after the home and children.

The Last Trials

The trials continued for many months. Anyone who dared to criticise them risked becoming a victim themselves. However, on 29 October 1692, Governor William Phips ordered the special court to close down. There were still many suspected witches in jail. So what brought an end to the witch trials?

Sir William Phips was the governor of the province of Massachusetts from 1692 to 1694.

DAMNING EVIDENCE

By October 1692, Governor William Phips knew that many people were unhappy with the court. He also knew that innocent people had been found guilty. Increase Mather had questioned the use of dreams and visions as evidence in trials. So Governor William Phips decided to replace the court with one that would not allow spectral evidence.

Think about it

One woman accused of witchcraft was the wife of the governor himself. Do you think this might have influenced his decision to close down the court?

NEW TRIALS

The trials restarted at the beginning of 1693. Thanks to the new rules, very few people were found guilty. By May 1693, the governor used a royal pardon to clear anyone suspected of witchcraft and release those still in prison.

COUNTING THE COST

Governor William Phips's decision came too late for many. More than 200 people were accused of being involved in witchcraft. In total, 20 people were executed between June and October 1692. Martha Corey was one of the last to be executed on 19 September 1692. Five other people died in prison.

This appeal is from 10 women and 3 or 4 men imprisoned on witchcraft charges. The appeal asks that they are released on bail over winter to stand trial in spring.

This picture imagines Giles Corey in prison, possibly with his wife Martha.

Repairing the Damage

The Salem witch trials ended in the spring of 1693. Everyone accused of witchcraft was released from prison. Laws were changed to ensure that the disaster of the Salem witch trials could never happen again. In the years that followed, some of the people involved apologised for their roles in the trials.

Judge Samuel Sewall

ENDING THE STORY

Over the years that followed, the authorities and people involved started to talk about the terrible events of 1692. Samuel Sewall, one of the judges from the special court, admitted that he had made mistakes during the trials. In Salem, arguments between the **opponents** and supporters of Minister Samuel Parris continued right until he left the village in 1697.

Samuel Sewall wrote in his diary about his regret for what had happened.

A **memorial** near Salem Village to remember the innocent.

Regni ANNÆ Reginæ Decimo.

Province of the Massachusetts-Bay.

AN ACT,

Made and Passed by the Great and General Court or Assembly of Her Majesty's Province of the Massachusetts-Bay in New-England, Held at Boston the 17th Day of October, 1711.

An Act to Reverse the Attainders of George Burroughs and others for Witchcraft.

NEXT STEPS

Ann Putnam accused many people of witchcraft. She later apologised for her actions. She said she had been misled by the Devil. Tituba was released from prison in 1693. But the rest of her life is a mystery. It is not known what happened to many of the accusers and victims of the trials.

In 1711, a law was passed in Massachusetts. It pardoned the people who were convicted of witchcraft during the Salem witch trials. As a result of this law, money was paid to the families of the victims.

CHANGING LAWS

The witch trials happened at a time when the legal and court systems of Massachusetts were going through a lot of changes. People assumed the victims were guilty, and the victims did not have the help of defence lawyers. The evidence used in the trials would never be **admissible** in a modern court. The disastrous mistakes made in the trials helped shape the future laws of the United States.

THE LAST WITCHES?

The Salem witch trials did not stop people from believing in witchcraft. However, putting suspected witches on trial became much rarer and soon ended in North America.

Fascinating fact

The families of the victims executed in Salem were given **compensation** after the pardons were issued. They received about £600, the equivalent of about £63,500 now. The money was paid in pounds sterling as Massachusetts was a British colony.

Lessons from History

The Salem witch trials were a tragedy for the victims and the whole community of Salem Village. But there were other witch trials in Colonial America at this time. And witch trials happened over many centuries across Europe. So why do we remember the events of Salem, and what can we learn from them?

COLONIAL AMERICA

Court documents tell us many details of the Salem witch trials. These documents are a window into the lives of people in colonial times. They show a community in crisis. Disagreements about religion, outsiders, and other issues caused **paranoia** about witchcraft.

PRESSURE TO CONFORM

Many of Salem's women were found guilty of being witches. This is likely to be because they did not act in the way society expected them to. This also applied to the men who were accused when they refused to join in the witch hunts. At that time, it was dangerous not to behave in the way that was expected.

The Crucible shows how quickly a community can become divided.

WHAT IS THE EVIDENCE?

Shockingly, people were put on trial based on the dreams or visions of their accusers. Today, courts need proof that something happened. While things have improved, the Salem events show how important it is to not pass judgment until all the facts are available.

A COMMUNITY TORN APART

In just a few weeks, Salem went from an unexplained illness to a crisis that tore a community apart and led to at least 25 innocent people losing their lives. In 1953, the writer Arthur Miller wrote a play called *The Crucible* based on what had happened in Salem. It was a strong message and a warning about how society can **persecute** people for their views.

Uncovering the Truth

A lot is known about the people and events of the Salem witch trials. This is because there are so many primary and secondary sources available. A primary source is a document or object created at the time of a historical event. A secondary source is a document or object created after the event, or by someone who was not directly involved in it. They can explain or interpret primary sources. They help in understanding an event.

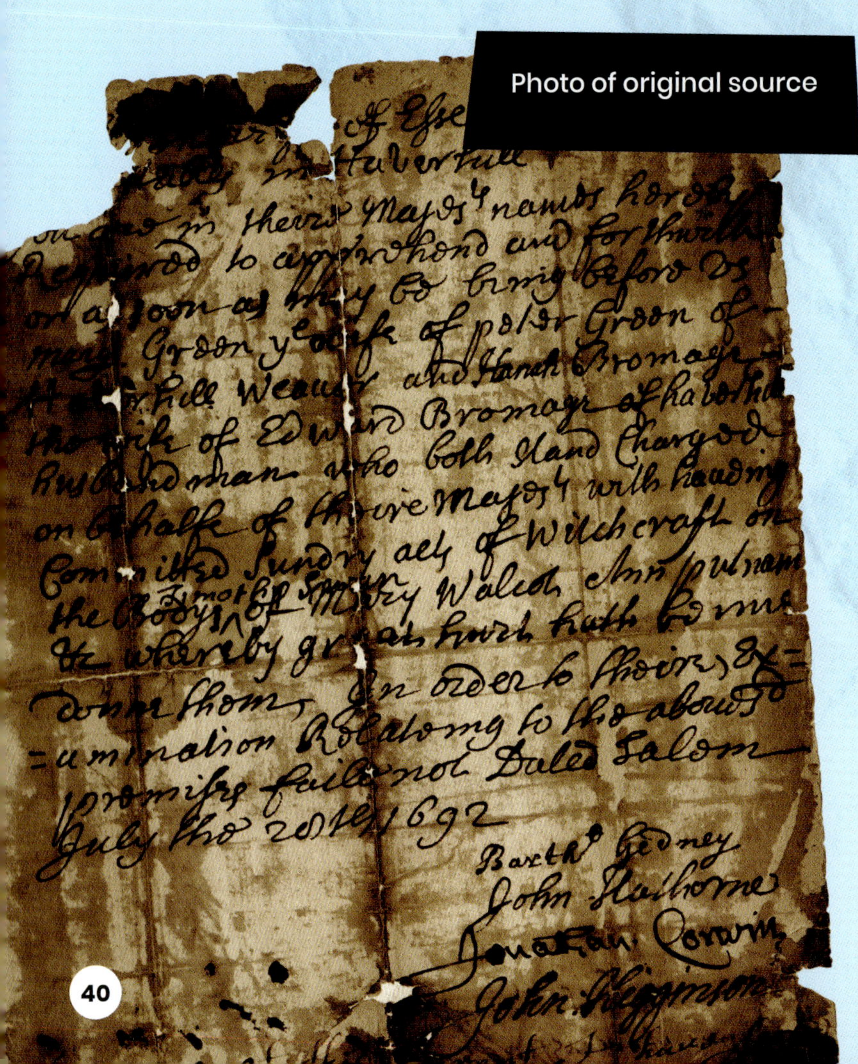

Photo of original source

Primary sources include

- official documents
- letters
- diaries
- paintings or drawings
- photographs
- sound recordings
- videos

Secondary sources include

- news articles
- books
- media documentaries
- encyclopaedias

DIFFERENT POINTS OF VIEW

Primary and secondary sources may tell different stories depending on the views of the people who created them. A victim of the Salem witch trials would have a different perspective from a judge. It is important to question sources – doing this helps us to understand them and understand different perspectives better.

ARREST WARRANT

This document is a primary source. It is an arrest warrant dating from 1692. The language in it dates from the time and can be quite difficult to understand now.

Original source text

[Y]ou are in theire Majests names hereby Required to apprehend and forthwith or as soon as may be bring before us. Mary. Green ye wife of peter Green of Haverhill Weaver and Hanah Bromage the wife of Edward Bromage of haverhil husbandman

You are ordered, as quickly as possible, to arrest Mary Green, the wife of the weaver Peter Green, and Hannah Bromage, the wife of the farmer Edward Bromage, both from Haverhill.

who both stand Charged on behalfe of theire Majests with haveing Committed Sundry acts of Witchcraft on the Bodys Timothy Swan of Mary Walcot Ann Putnam & whereby great hurt hath benne donne them,

They are accused of using witchcraft to hurt Timothy Swan, Mary Walcott and Ann Putnam.

In order to theire, Examination Relateing to the abovesd premises faile not

Bring them to us as soon as possible so we can question them about these charges.

Dated Salem July the 28th 1692

Salem, 28 July 1692

Look at the arrest warrant, then read the transcribed, annotated version of the text and answer the questions below.

Quick questions

- Who are the two people being accused of witchcraft?
- What was the purpose of this document?
- What was the word used at this time for a farmer?

Discussion questions

- Do you think the person who wrote this document necessarily believed that the accused were guilty?
- Why do you think the two women were accused of witchcraft but not their husbands?
- Why do you think this document might have survived when a lot of written documents of the time didn't?

- Mary Green and Hannah Bromage.
- It was an order to arrest Mary Green and Hannah Bromage.
- A husbandman.

Vocabulary Builder
Turmoil in Salem

How would the Salem witch trials be reported today? Read this fictional article to see how a newspaper might cover the story. Pay attention to key words that describe the investigation and how local people are reacting to it.

WITCH TRIALS SHAKE SALEM

People across the state of Massachusetts are shocked by the witch trials taking place in Salem Village. They started when a young woman became ill with a mystery illness. A local doctor said she was bewitched. Members of the prominent Putnam family have been affected by the strange illness.

Since the first arrests, accusations have spread throughout the village. Many women and some men have been accused of being witches.

In response to the crisis, the state governor William Phips has set up a special court. Much of the evidence consists of what the accusers have seen in dreams and visions. Some people are worried this is not strong enough to prove guilt. But some judges think it should be examined in court.

The people of Salem Village are very concerned about what is happening. They hope these trials will reveal the cause of their community's problems.

Imagine you are reporting on the Salem witch trials for a newspaper. Then use the report on page 42 and the prompts and word bank below to write your own news story.

- **What is happening?**
- **How do people feel?**
- **What details can you add to interest readers?**

Looking at evidence	accusations, examine, identify, investigate, question, suspicion, witness
Reactions	alarmed, disturbed, scared, shocked, suspicious, upset, worried
Descriptions	extraordinary, frightening, mystery, prominent, serious, sinister

Glossary

Accused A person who has been charged with doing something morally wrong or illegal.

Admissible Acceptable or valid as evidence in a court of law.

Archaeological evidence Anything from the past that has been left behind by the people who lived then. This might include tools, clothes, pottery or even bones.

Bewitched To be put under a spell or other form of witchcraft, which often makes someone act differently.

Biased To have a negative opinion about someone or something without good reason.

Charge An accusation made against someone saying they did something against the law.

Colony An area or region that is governed by another country.

Commit To do something, especially something wrong like a crime.

Compensation Something, usually money, awarded to a person in recognition of loss, suffering or injury.

Condemned To be found guilty and punished for a crime.

Confess To admit to doing something wrong or against the law.

Critical Pointing out someone's faults or shortcomings.

Defence lawyer Someone who represents and defends individuals or organisations accused of a crime.

Defer To let someone else make decisions.

Deputy Constable A person who helps make sure the law is followed.

Devil The evil force in the Christian religion.

Diagnosis The process of finding out what is causing an illness or disease.

Disprove To show that something is untrue.

Dominated To be controlled by someone or something.

Enslaved To be forced to work for someone else without the freedom to stop or leave.

Evidence Information that can be used as proof to show whether something is true or false.

Executed To be put to death as punishment for a crime.

Fits Sudden and uncontrollable body movements, often caused by illness.

Gallows A large wooden frame with a rope that was used to hang criminals as punishment.

Governed To be ruled or controlled by a leader or government.

Governor The head of government in a US state or territory.

Grudge A long-standing feeling of anger towards someone because of something they did in the past.

Indigenous Indigenous peoples are groups of people who are the original inhabitants of a region or area. There may be many different groups of Indigenous peoples within a region, each with their own languages and cultures.

Innkeeper A person who owns or runs a place where travellers can stay.

Innocent To not be guilty of a crime or any wrongdoing; someone who has done nothing wrong.

Judge A person who is in charge of a trial in a court and decides how a person who is guilty of a crime should be punished, or who makes decisions on legal matters.

Lord's Prayer A well-known Christian prayer that is used as an example of how to pray.

Mass hysteria When a group of people develop similar symptoms that do not have an identifiable physical cause.

Magistrate A person who has the power to make decisions about the law and punish others.

Medieval The historical period of time starting in the 400s and ending in the 1400s.

Memorial Something created to remember a person or event.

Minister An official of the Christian church who often leads religious services.

New England The American colonial region of the northeast, consisting of what are now the states of Maine, Vermont, New Hampshire, Massachusetts, Connecticut and Rhode Island.

Offence An action that breaks a rule or law.

Official A person who represents an institution, such as a court, and has the power to make decisions.

Opponent Someone who is against another person in an argument.

Opposed To be against or in disagreement with something, such as an idea or action.

Outraged To be angered or upset about something that is unfair or wrong.

Paranoia Intense and irrational fear, distrust and suspicion without any evidence or good reason.

Pardon To forgive someone for a crime, removing their punishment.

Persecute To treat someone badly and unfairly because of their beliefs or actions.

Puritans A group of very strict English Protestants, many of whom moved to the American colonies in the 1600s and 1700s.

Right Something that allows someone to do or have something, such as the right to have a fair trial. Rights are usually protected by law.

Settlers A group of people who move away from one area to live in a new one.

Source A written document, artefact or building that provides information relating to the past. Sources are also known as evidence.

Supernatural Something outside of or beyond the natural world, such as magic or ghosts.

Suspicion A feeling that something might be possible, likely or true, or that something might be happening (whether good or bad).

Trial A legal meeting held in court where people decide if someone is guilty or innocent of an offence.

Vision A sight seen in one's mind. It can also mean seeing something that is not really there.

Witchcraft The practice of using magic or spells, often believed to be done by witches.

Worship To act in a way that shows great respect and/or love for someone. People often worship God. The word is frequently used to describe church services.

Index

Acknowledgments

The publisher would like to thank the following for their kind permission to reproduce their photographs:

(Key: a-above; b-below/bottom; c-centre; f-far; l-left; r-right; t-top)

4 Alamy Stock Photo: Classic Image (bl). **4-5 Alamy Stock Photo:** North Wind Picture Archives (t). **6 Alamy Stock Photo:** Everett Collection Historical (bl); North Wind Picture Archives (cr). **7 Alamy Stock Photo:** FLHC DBM1 (bl); The Picture Art Collection (cl). **8 Alamy Stock Photo:** Granger Historical Picture Archive (br). **9 Alamy Stock Photo:** The History Collection (br). **Bridgeman Images:** Granger (tl). **10-11 Alamy Stock Photo:** Granger Historical Picture Archive (t); The History Collection (b). **11 Alamy Stock Photo:** Steven Milne (cr). **12 Getty Images:** Bettmann (tr); mikroman6 (bl). **13 Alamy Stock Photo:** North Wind Picture Archives (bl, br). **14 Alamy Stock Photo:** Science History Images (bl); World History Archive (tr). **15 Alamy Stock Photo:** The Granger Collection (t, b). **16 Alamy Stock Photo:** Granger Historical Picture Archive (tr); North Wind Picture Archives (b). **17 Alamy Stock Photo:** North Wind Picture Archives (t). **Getty Images:** Kean Collection (b). **18 Alamy Stock Photo:** Granger Historical Picture Archive (bl). **Getty Images:** Print Collector (tr). **19 Alamy Stock Photo:** Everett Collection Historical (tr); North Wind Picture Archives (tl); Granger Historical Picture Archive (cl). **20 Alamy Stock Photo:** Everett Collection Historical (b); The Picture Art Collection (tr). **21 Alamy Stock Photo:** Classic Image (br); Old Paper Studios (tl); Pictorial Press Ltd (tc). **Peabody Essex Museum:** Phillips Library (bl). **26 Alamy Stock Photo:** Chronicle (tr); North Wind Picture Archives (b). **27 Alamy Stock Photo:** Penta Springs Limited (t); World History Archive (c). **Bridgeman Images:** North Wind Pictures (br). **28 Alamy Stock Photo:** FLHC MADB1 (bl). **Getty Images:** CBS Photo Archive (t). **29 Alamy Stock Photo:** Classic Image (b). **30 Alamy Stock Photo:** Classic Image. **31 Alamy Stock Photo:** Pictorial Press Ltd (t). **Getty Images:** Print Collector (cr). **Peabody Essex Museum:** Phillips Library (bl). **32 Shutterstock.com:** Mike Seberger (b). **33 Alamy Stock Photo:** ClassicStock (b); The Print Collector (t). **34 Alamy Stock Photo:** Universal Images Group North America LLC (r). **35 Bridgeman Images:** (br). **Library of Congress, Washington, D.C.:** (tl). **36 Bridgeman Images:** Massachusetts Historical Society (c). **Collection of the Massachusetts Historical Society:** www.masshist.org/database/23125852_sewall_p113_work_lg (br). **37 Alamy Stock Photo:** Maurice Savage (t). **Library of Congress, Washington, D.C.. 38 Alamy Stock Photo:** Everett Collection Historical (t). **Bridgeman Images:** The New York Historical (b). **39 Alamy Stock Photo:** Donald Cooper (b); Granger Historical Picture Archive (t). **40 William L. Clements Library, The University Of Michigan:** Women, Gender, and Family Collection (bl). **43 Getty Images:** mikroman6 (t).

Cover images: Front: **Getty Images / iStock:** glegorly bl, ThomasOsborne t; **Shutterstock.com:** Georgios Antonatos br, Everett Collection c; Back: **Alamy Stock Photo:** The Granger Collection t, North Wind Picture Archives c, b.

Quote attributions:

Hale, John. 1702. *Modest Enquiry into the Nature of Witchcraft*. Applewood Books.
Mather, Cotton. 1693. *The Wonders of the Invisible World*. John Dunstan.
Mather, Increase. 1693. *Cases of Conscience Concerning Evil Spirits*. Benjamin Harris.

All the books in the DK Super History series have been reviewed by authenticity readers to ensure the represented cultures and experiences are accurate.

This book uses language as appropriate to modern contexts. Historical terms that are no longer acceptable may be present in original source materials and images. These sources are included to present authentic insights into history.